THE R ASTLEY EXPERIENCE

THE LIFE AND TIMES OF RICK ASTLEY

All rights reserved. No part of this publication may be reproduced, distributed, or transmitted in any form or by any means, including photocopying, recording, or other electronic or mechanical methods, without the prior written permission of the publisher, except in the case of brief quotations embodied in critical reviews and certain other noncommercial uses permitted by copyright law.

Copyright ©Amanda R. Branson 2023.

TABLE OF CONTENTS

CHAPTER 1

WHO IS RICK ASTLEY

CHAPTER 2

EARLY LIFE

CHAPTER 3

CAREER

CHAPTER 4

INTERESTING THINGS ABOUT

CHAPTER 1

WHO IS RICK ASTLEY

Rick Astley is an English singer, songwriter, and musician who was born in Newton-le-Willows, Lancashire, England on February 6, 1966. He rose to global fame in the late 1980s with his smash hit song "Never Gonna Give You Up," which topped the charts in many countries. His unique, deep voice and memorable pop songs, such as "Together Forever," "Whenever You Need Somebody," and "She Wants to Dance with Me," have made him a successful musician.

In the mid-1990s, Astley decided to take a break from music, but he was thrust back into the spotlight in the 2000s due to the online fad known as "Rickrolling." People on the internet would trick others into clicking a link that would take them to the "Never Gonna Give You Up" music video. This viral fad made Astley's music accessible to a younger audience and kept him in the public eye.

Since then, Rick Astley has kept up his music releases and live performances. He has a devoted following and is still regarded as a 1980s pop star. His music combines pop, dance, and soul elements, and his mellow voice remains his defining feature.

Rick Astley has carried on releasing new songs and performing on tour ever since his fame began to rise again. He has released a number of albums, including "50" in 2016—his first studio album in more than a decade. Positive reviews aided the album's ascension to number one on the UK Albums Chart.

Beyond his well-known tunes from the 1980s, Astley has had success. He has shown his artistic diversity by experimenting with his sound and exploring other musical genres. His subsequent recordings, including "Beautiful Life" (2018) and "The Best of Me" (2019), demonstrate a fusion of pop, soul, and modern elements.

Rick Astley has dabbled in a variety of endeavors outside of music. He has worked with many musicians, appeared on television programs, and supported charitable causes. He has received recognition for his services to the music business, including various awards and nominations.

The ageless nature of Rick Astley's music is shown by his everlasting appeal. His unusual voice and memorable songs have elevated him to a cherished position in popular culture. Astley never fails to wow audiences with his brilliance and charisma, whether it be via his earlier albums or his timeless songs.

CHAPTER 2

EARLY LIFE

Rick Astley had a strong interest in music from a young age. He started playing the drums at a young age and often performed at bars and clubs in the area. Astley developed a passion for singing and worked on his vocal abilities while playing in various bands. When he was in his late teens and working as a driver for a delivery service, Pete Waterman, a record producer, discovered him. Waterman signed Astley to PWL, a newly established record company, and his musical career began. In 1987, Astley released his first song,

"Never Gonna Give You Up," and it quickly became a global hit, topping the charts in 25 countries. This was followed by other singles such as "Whenever You Need Somebody," "Together Forever," and "She Wants to Dance with Me." Despite his sudden fame, Astley kept a low profile and focused on his music career, releasing three studio albums. In 1993, he decided to step away from the music industry and spend more time with his family.

Astley married his long-time partner, Lene Bausager, and they had a daughter together. In 2007, Astley made a comeback to the music scene after more than a decade. The "Rickrolling" meme, which involved people being directed to the music video for "Never Gonna Give You Up" as a joke, increased his online profile. This led to a renewed interest in his music and Astley began touring and releasing new songs. His albums, including "50" in 2016 and "Beautiful Life" in 2018, were all well-received. Astley's deep voice and memorable tunes have made him a pop music legend.

In addition to his solo projects, Astley has collaborated with other musicians. In 2008, he worked with the German dance music duo Cascada on a remix of "Never Gonna Give You Up," introducing his song to a new audience. His music has also been featured in movies, TV shows, and advertisements. Astley's seventh studio album, "The Best of Me," was released in 2019 and included new songs as well as remastered versions of his biggest hits. The album was praised and showed Astley's artistic range. He has also been praised for his energetic live performances and his ability to connect with his audience.

Rick Astley has had a huge influence on mainstream culture and his songs and personality have become iconic. He is still active in the music industry and continues to put out new songs, demonstrating his love of music. Astley has adopted a more sophisticated sound while still staying true to his pop roots, showing his artistic growth. He is known for his humble nature and has expressed his gratitude for the support of his fans. Astley has been an inspiration to other performers and is still a popular figure in the music industry.

PERSONAL LIFE

In 1988, Rick Astley tied the knot with Lene Bausager, a Danish movie producer. They have one daughter, Emilie, who was born in 1992. In interviews, Astley has highlighted the importance of striking a balance between his personal and professional lives. He has also expressed his love and devotion to his family, which includes a brother and two sisters. Rick Jr. is the son of Rick Astley from his first marriage to Carol. He has stressed the importance of maintaining a balance between his work and family life, as well as his fondness for his family.

PERSONALITY

Rick Astley is often described as humble and down-to-earth, despite his success in the music industry. He has kept a low-key and friendly attitude throughout his career, and is known for his good-natured attitude and sense of humor. His success is a testament to his hard work and dedication, as he has been making music and performing live shows since the 1980s. His passion for music is evident in his performances and the emotion he brings to his songs. He values his privacy and prefers a more modest lifestyle, and is reflective and thoughtful in interviews.

Rick Astley is genuine and sincere in his interactions, and his music often conveys a positive and optimistic outlook. He is resilient and adaptable, and is appreciative of his fans and their support. He is family-oriented and loves music of all genres, and is humble and gracious in his interactions with others. He is versatile and open to experimentation, and is an engaging and charismatic performer. He is also modest and unpretentious, and is known for being friendly and approachable. Finally, he has a strong work ethic and is committed to creating quality music.

HOBBIES AND PASTIMES

Rick Astley is a well-known singer, songwriter, and musician from England who made a big impact on the pop music genre in the late 1980s with his hit song "Never Gonna Give You Up". Although the specifics of his hobbies and interests are not widely known, here are some activities he may enjoy:

1. Music: As a professional musician, Rick Astley is likely passionate about music. He probably spends time composing songs, exploring different musical genres, and staying up to date with the latest musical trends.

2. Performances: Throughout his career, Astley has given many live performances. He likely enjoys engaging with his audience while performing on stage, as well as attending other musicians' concerts.

3. Songwriting: Astley has written and collaborated on some of his own tracks. He may find songwriting to be a fun pastime, as it allows for creative expression and storytelling.

4. Fitness and Sports: Rick Astley is known for his love of fitness and sports. Although the exact activities he takes part in are not known, it is likely that he exercises to stay healthy and active.

5. Family Time: Astley probably values spending time with his family. He could enjoy participating in family-friendly activities and making lasting memories with his loved ones.

6. Travel: As a popular artist, Astley has had the opportunity to visit many countries and perform for audiences around the world. He may enjoy discovering new places, learning about other cultures, and experiencing the joys of travel.

7. Other Interests: Astley may have other personal interests or hobbies that are kept private. Just like anyone else, he could have a wide range of interests and pastimes.

8. Photography: Astley may be interested in photography. Many people enjoy taking pictures and seeing the world through a camera's lens. He could appreciate using photography to capture his experiences when he travels and encounters new things.

9. Cooking and Culinary Exploration: Astley could have a liking for cooking and experimenting with different cuisines. His favorite activities could include trying out new foods, hosting get-togethers for friends and family, and exploring other cuisines.

10. Outdoor Activities: Astley may enjoy going on hikes, bike rides, or even gardening. Being outside and engaging in outdoor activities can be

therapeutic, physically active, and a way to connect with nature.

11. Philanthropic Work: Throughout his career, Astley has taken part in many philanthropic endeavors. He has contributed to causes such as Children in Need and Nordoff Robbins, a nonprofit that promotes music therapy. He may find great satisfaction in giving back to the community and participating in charitable endeavors.

12. Reading: Astley could find pleasure in reading books for pleasure and professional development. Reading can be enjoyable, mentally stimulating, and a way to escape to other worlds. He may have a preference for certain writers or genres.

13. Technology and Gadgets: Astley could be interested in technology and gadgets due to his career's connection to the music industry and the ever-changing technological world. His interests could include discovering new technology, keeping

up with technological developments, and playing with various digital tools.

14. Film and TV: As an entertainer and performer, Astley may have an affinity for these media. He could enjoy watching movies, experimenting with different genres, and watching TV shows.

15. Personal Development: Astley may be interested in improving his character. Learning new skills, practicing mindfulness, and engaging in other pursuits can all contribute to personal development and wellbeing.

RECOGNIZE

Rick Astley has been a major figure in the music industry for decades, with his recognitions ranging from his initial success in the late 1980s to his continued relevance and influence in the digital age. His signature song, "Never Gonna Give You Up," released in 1987, topped the charts in 25 countries and became one of the best-selling singles of all time. Its music video, featuring the iconic "Rickrolling" meme, gained widespread popularity on the internet, further solidifying Astley's fame. He has received several awards throughout his career, including the Brit Award for Best British Single in 1988 for "Never Gonna Give You Up" and a Grammy Award nomination in 1989 in the category of Best New Artist. Astley has released multiple successful albums, including his debut album "Whenever You Need Somebody" (1987), which reached number one in the UK and spawned several hit singles. His other albums, such as "Hold Me in Your Arms" (1988) and "Free" (1991), also achieved commercial success. While his popularity waned in the 1990s, he made a comeback in the 2000s and has continued to release new music. His album "50" (2016) debuted at number one on the UK Albums Chart, becoming his first chart-topping album in almost three decades. Due to the unexpected popularity of "Rickrolling," Astley gained a new wave of internet fame in the mid-2000s. The

"Rickrolling" phenomenon involved tricking internet users into clicking on a disguised link that led to the music video of "Never Gonna Give You Up." It became an internet meme and achieved viral status. Astley's music has had a lasting impact on popular culture, with "Never Gonna Give You Up" being referenced and parodied in various forms of media, including television shows, films, and advertisements. His unique baritone voice and catchy pop tunes have made him an enduring figure in the music industry.

CHAPTER 3

CAREER

Rick Astley's journey to fame was a remarkable one. In 1985, Pete Waterman, a record producer, discovered Astley while he was playing drums in a few local bands. Waterman was impressed by Astley's talent and signed him to PWL Records, a renowned British record label that specializes in dance-pop music. Astley's first single, "Never Gonna Give You Up," was released in 1987 and quickly became a global hit, topping the charts in many countries. The song's catchy chorus, memorable melody, and Astley's soulful, deep voice resonated with listeners everywhere.

In 1987, Astley released his first album, "Whenever You Need Somebody," which was a huge success, topping the charts in the United Kingdom and producing multiple hit singles, such as "Together Forever" and "It Would Take a Strong, Strong Man." Astley's music was also well-received abroad, particularly in the United States, where "Never Gonna Give You Up" peaked at number one on the Billboard Hot 100 list. His unique voice and the energetic dancing he displayed in his music videos were key factors in his success as a worldwide pop star.

Throughout the late 1980s and early 1990s, Astley continued to release new music, although his subsequent albums did not achieve the same level of commercial success as his first. However, they still had hit songs and kept his devoted fan base. In the 2000s, Astley experienced a resurgence in popularity due to the "Rickrolling" internet phenomenon. The joke used deceptive links that took unsuspecting internet users to the "Never Gonna Give You Up" music video, which exposed his classic song to a whole new audience.

Rick Astley's climb to fame was propelled by his unique voice, catchy pop tunes, and passionate fan base. His music had a lasting impact on society, and "Never Gonna Give You Up" is still a renowned song today. Astley's period of greatest success was in the late 1980s, when he released his breakthrough song "Never Gonna Give You Up" and the subsequent album "Whenever You Need Somebody." During this time, Astley achieved great fame and acclaim.

Astley became an overnight pop phenomenon when the song's popularity propelled him into the limelight.

2. Chart dominance: Astley's 1987 first album, "Whenever You Need Somebody," was a huge commercial success. It succeeded well overseas and reached the top of the charts in the United Kingdom, where it was certified platinum. The album gave rise to a number of successful songs, such as "Never Gonna Give You Up," "Together

Forever," and "It Would Take a Strong, Strong Man."

3. Recognition Abroad: Astley's success went beyond his own country. In the US, where "Never Gonna Give You Up" peaked at number one on the Billboard Hot 100 list, he had great success. Because his music connected with listeners all across the world, Astley developed a devoted following.

4. Concerts and Tours: During the height of his popularity, Rick Astley took part in a number of concert tours and gave countless live performances. His charismatic stage appearance, together with his unusual voice and dancing routines, enthralled audiences and further cemented his reputation as a sought-after performer.

5. Lasting Legacy: Despite Astley's monetary success as measured by chart performance declining in the years that followed, his music and

the cultural effect of "Never Gonna Give You Up" persisted. The song became a mainstay of '80s nostalgia and saw a resurgence of popularity in the 2000s thanks to online memes and the "Rickrolling" craze, ensuring that Astley's name remained well-known even to newer generations. Rick Astley's worldwide pop stardom was secured at his career's pinnacle in the late 1980s. His long influence on popular culture was largely attributed to his distinctive voice, appealing melodies, and captivating performances.

CHAPTER 4

INTERESTING THINGS ABOUT

Rick Astley is an English singer, songwriter, and musician who achieved worldwide fame in the late 1980s with his hit song "Never Gonna Give You Up." Here are some interesting facts about him: Rick was born on February 6, 1966, in Newton-le-Willows, Lancashire, England. He started his music career as a drummer in local bands before being discovered by the record producer Pete Waterman. His debut single, "Never Gonna Give You Up," was released in 1987 and became a global success, topping the charts in 25 countries. The song became even more popular in the internet age due to the creation of the "Rickrolling" meme, where the music video for "Never Gonna Give You Up" would be disguised as something else and unsuspecting internet users would be redirected to it. His debut album, "Whenever You Need Somebody," was released the same year and was also a huge success, selling over 15 million copies worldwide. He won the 1988 Brit Award for Best British Single for "Never Gonna Give You Up." Astley's deep voice and energetic dance moves became his signature style and contributed to his popularity.

Despite his initial success, Astley retired from the music industry in 1993 at the age of 27, citing exhaustion and a desire for a more private life. He made a comeback in 2007 when "Never Gonna Give You Up" gained renewed popularity through the Rickrolling meme. In recent years, Astley has released new music and continues to perform live. He has released several albums, including "50" in 2016 and "Beautiful Life" in 2018. His music style is influenced by a variety of genres, including pop, soul, and dance music. He has sold over 40 million records worldwide throughout his career and has toured extensively, performing in concerts and music festivals around the world. In addition to his music career, Astley has also worked as a radio presenter and hosted his own show on Magic 105.4 in the UK.

Rick Astley has been a major influence in the music industry for over three decades. In 2008, he won the MTV Europe Music Award for Best Act Ever, thanks to the Rickrolling meme. His music has been covered by various musicians, and he has been cited as an influence by artists such as Bruno Mars and Foo Fighters. Despite his association with the meme, Astley has embraced it and has a good sense of humor about it. He even participated in live Rickroll performances and made appearances related to the meme.

In 2016, Astley released a new single titled "Keep Singing," which marked his first new release in over a decade. The song received positive reviews and showcased his enduring vocal talent. His music videos are known for their vibrant and energetic performances, often featuring him dancing and showcasing his smooth moves. He has performed at various notable events and venues, including the Macy's Thanksgiving Day Parade in the United States and the Glastonbury Festival in the UK.

Astley has released a total of 10 studio albums, including compilations and special editions. In 2019, he released a cover of the song "Everlong" by the Foo Fighters, putting his own spin on the alternative rock hit. He has been recognized with numerous awards throughout his career, including several Gold and Platinum certifications for his albums.

Rick Astley is known for his down-to-earth and humble personality, which has endeared him to fans and helped him maintain a loyal following. He has embarked on multiple successful tours, both solo and as a part of special events or collaborations with other artists. He also released his autobiography, titled "Rick Astley: The Autobiography," in 2018, which offers insights into his life and career. Astley has used his platform for charitable endeavors, supporting various causes over the years, including Children in Need and the Nordoff Robbins music therapy charity.

Printed in Great Britain
by Amazon